Babies

BY Deborah Heiligman   ILLUSTRATED BY Laura Freeman

SCHOLASTIC INC.
New York Toronto London Auckland Sydney
Mexico City New Delhi Hong Kong Buenos Aires

For my babies,
Aaron and Benjamin DH

To Milo,
my new baby LF

Everyone starts out as a baby. You were a baby once. Your mom and dad were babies, too. Even your grandparents were babies. You've grown and changed in many ways since you were a baby. Try putting on your baby clothes now....

DIAPERS

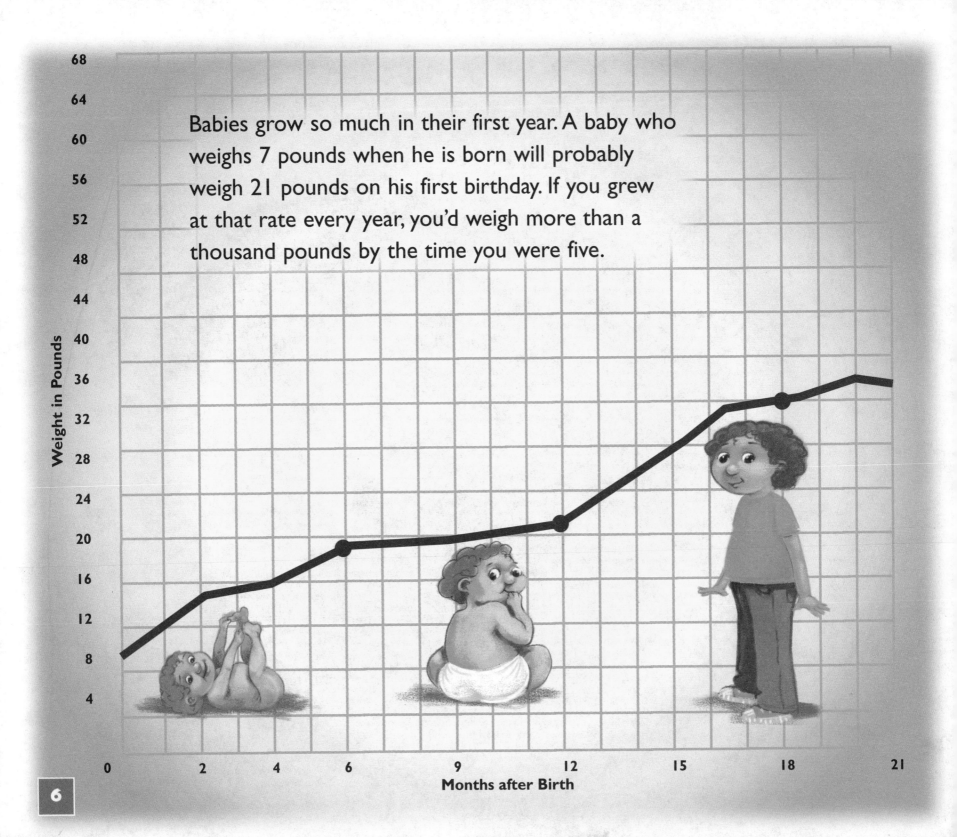

Babies grow so much in their first year. A baby who weighs 7 pounds when he is born will probably weigh 21 pounds on his first birthday. If you grew at that rate every year, you'd weigh more than a thousand pounds by the time you were five.

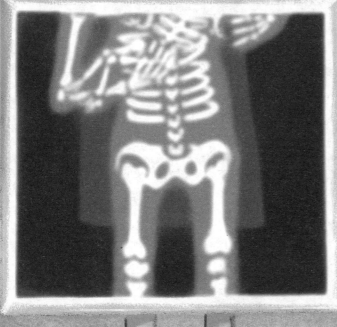

Newborn babies have more bones than grown-ups do. As babies grow, their bones grow and join together. A baby has six soft spots on his head where the bones have not joined yet. These bones join by the time he is a year and a half old. As babies grow, their bones get stronger, too. Your bones are still growing and getting stronger.

Babies change in other ways during their first year and a half. When babies are first born, they are helpless. They can't walk or talk. They can only breathe, blink, suck, swallow, sneeze, hiccup, and cry. These actions are called reflexes. A reflex is something you do automatically. Besides sleeping, that's about all newborn babies do. Oh, and go in their diapers.

Newborn babies can't take care of themselves. But they can communicate that they need help. How do they communicate? They cry.

When you want a cookie, you say, "May I please have a cookie?"

When a baby is hungry, he says, *"Waaaaaa!"*

Moms and dads and big brothers and sisters learn the difference between the cry that means "Feed me" and the cry that means "Hold me" and the cry that means "Get me out of this diaper!"

Even though babies can't do much, they know a lot more than you might think.

A newborn baby can recognize his mother's voice as soon as he is born. A few days later he can already recognize voices of other people who spend a lot of time with him, such as his father, his big brother, and his big sister.

A baby who is only ten days old can already tell the difference between his mother's smell and someone else's.

Scientists also have found that new babies can
taste the difference between sweet and bitter and sour.
They can't taste salt, though.
Can you guess which taste a newborn baby likes best?
Sweet! Mother's milk is sweet.

A baby's eyesight changes as the baby grows. In the beginning, babies don't see color. They do by the time they are about four months old. So newborns like to look at black-and-white pictures and toys.

But a baby's favorite thing to look at is a human face, especially one he is getting to know well. A baby's eyes can focus best on a face that is 10 or 12 inches away—the distance between your face and the baby's when you hold him in your arms.

When we look at a baby, we can often see that the baby looks like a member of the family. That's because babies get their looks from moms, dads, grandparents, aunts, uncles, and other relatives on the family tree. Who do you look like?

Babies who are adopted get their looks from their birth parents. But as they grow up, they do many things like the parents who are raising them, and like their brothers and sisters.

Sometimes a mom gives birth to two babies at the same time. These are twins. Some twins look almost exactly alike. They're called identical twins. Identical twins are either both boys or both girls.

Some twins don't look exactly alike. These are called fraternal twins. Fraternal twins can be one boy and one girl, or two boys, or two girls.

18

Once in a while a mom gives birth to
3 babies,
4 babies,
5 babies, or even
6 babies.

So far, the most babies a mom ever gave birth to was seven.

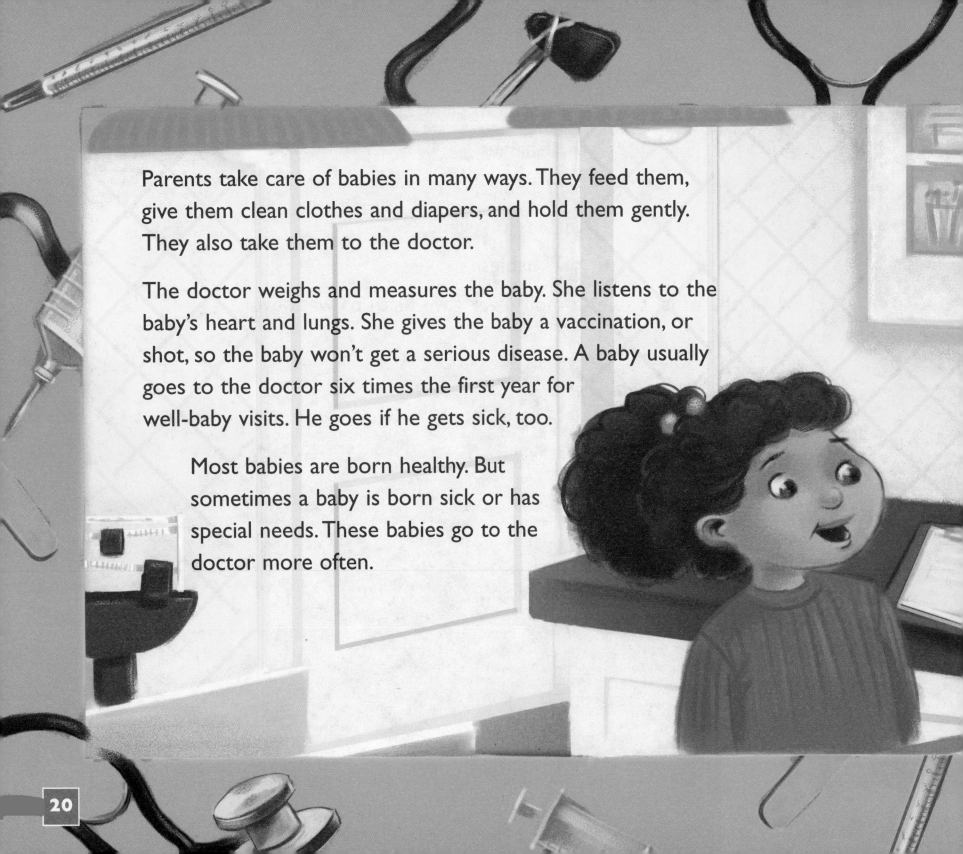

Parents take care of babies in many ways. They feed them, give them clean clothes and diapers, and hold them gently. They also take them to the doctor.

The doctor weighs and measures the baby. She listens to the baby's heart and lungs. She gives the baby a vaccination, or shot, so the baby won't get a serious disease. A baby usually goes to the doctor six times the first year for well-baby visits. He goes if he gets sick, too.

Most babies are born healthy. But sometimes a baby is born sick or has special needs. These babies go to the doctor more often.

In the beginning taking care of a baby can be very tiring. Newborn babies sleep a lot—sometimes as much as 16 or 18 hours a day. But they sleep only a little bit at a time—even at night. Babies wake up when they need to be fed. And since their tummies are tiny, they need to be fed often—every two or three or four hours. Day or night. As a baby gets older, he sleeps more at night and less during the day.

What do new babies eat? Hamburgers? Corn on the cob? Sushi? Pasta? No! For the first few months of a baby's life, a baby drinks milk. Mother's milk is full of the vitamins and nutrients a baby needs. Sometimes a baby drinks formula, which is made to be like mother's milk.

A new baby's body is not ready for the food you eat. A baby's tongue and cheek muscles work together to suck liquid but not to swallow food. The baby's stomach is not ready for food either.

When babies are five or six months old, parents give them mushy foods like baby cereal, applesauce, and mashed bananas. When babies are a little older and may have some teeth, they eat pieces of food such as crackers, meat, or cheese. The pieces have to be very small so that babies don't choke on their food.

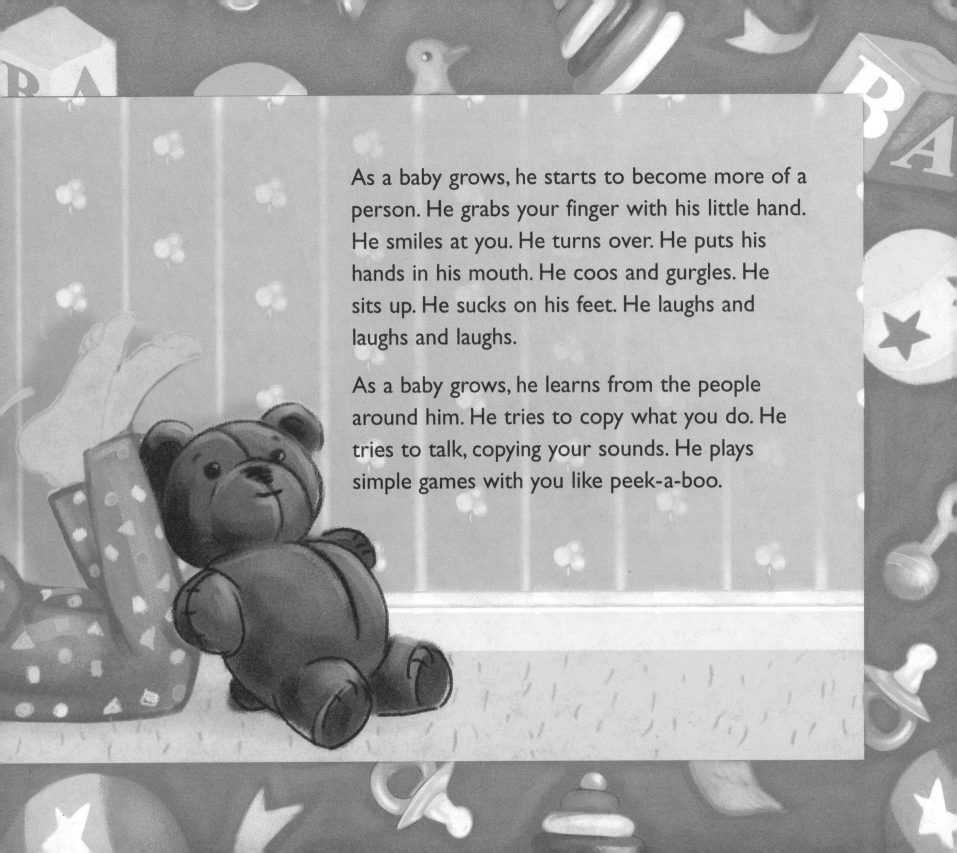

As a baby grows, he starts to become more of a person. He grabs your finger with his little hand. He smiles at you. He turns over. He puts his hands in his mouth. He coos and gurgles. He sits up. He sucks on his feet. He laughs and laughs and laughs.

As a baby grows, he learns from the people around him. He tries to copy what you do. He tries to talk, copying your sounds. He plays simple games with you like peek-a-boo.

Around the time of a baby's first birthday, he will start to walk and say a few words. But babies do things their own ways and at different times. Most babies crawl before they walk. But some babies don't ever crawl. Some babies talk before they walk. Other babies walk before they talk.

By the time a baby is about a year
and a half old, he really doesn't look
or act like a baby any more.

It's time to say bye-bye to the baby.

"Bye-bye, baby!"

"Hello, toddler!"

Be a Baby Scientist

Scientists study babies to find out what they know and what they can do. You can be a baby scientist, too.

Here's what you'll need:
- A baby
- A grown-up to help
- Paper and pencil to make an observation chart

Does baby imitate?

Age of baby: _____

Notes:

	Yes	No	
stick out tongue?	☐	☐	_____
Open and close hand?	☐	☐	_____

① Set up your chart. (See our example.)

② Get your baby's attention by talking to him in a sing-song, high voice. Have the grown-up help you.

③ Make sure the baby can see what you're doing. Stick out your tongue. Repeat ten times.

④ Does the baby imitate you? Put a check under "yes" or "no" on your chart. Write down any other observations, such as "his tongue came out part way" or "he yawned, too."

⑤ Now, try the experiment again. This time, open and close your hand. See if the baby imitates you.

What did you discover? (use a mirror to read)

Babies like to imitate, and they learn by imitating. As a baby gets older he can do more. Keep your observation chart and repeat this experiment as your baby gets older. You can have the baby imitate other things, too. Clap, play peek-a-boo, or make sounds. Does the baby do what you do?

The artist created her art by scanning her sketches and applying color to them on the computer.

Book design by LeSales Dunworth
The text is set in Gill Sans. The display type is Sawdust Marionette.

Jump Into Science series consultant: Christine Kiel, Early Education Science Specialist

The author and the publisher warmly thank Alice S. Carter, Ph.D., Associate Professor, University of Massachusetts, Boston, Department of Psychology, and Laurie S. Miller, Ph.D., Associate Professor of Psychiatry, Director, Institute for Children at Risk, NYU Child Study Center, for their assistance in reviewing the manuscript and artwork. The author also gratefully acknowledges Olwen Jarvis, Judy Heggestad, Dr. Tom Fitzpatrick, and Jinki Fitzpatrick.

Text copyright © 2002 by Deborah Heiligman.
Illustrations copyright © 2002 by Laura Freeman-Hines.
All rights reserved. Published by Scholastic Inc., 557 Broadway, New York, NY 10012, by arrangement with the National Geographic Society.
Printed in the U.S.A.

ISBN 0-439-84254-9